Greater Success Is Within Your Reach!

Let this book show you how to:

★ Use your time better
★ Realize your full potential
★ Develop better habits
★ Make a good impression
★ Build self-confidence
★ Conquer stressful situations
★ Solve problems more quickly and easily
★ Get the best out of life for you and yours
★ Be better organized
★ Find inner peace and happiness
★ Overcome fear, fatigue, and worry
★ Relax your mind and body
★ Achieve business and personal goals
★ Understand others and work well with them
★ Hone your communication skills
★ Improve yourself . . . and your life.

JUST TURN THIS PAGE . . .

ONE-MINUTE THOUGHTS That Bring WISDOM HARMONY and FULFILLMENT

Richard and Janet Budzik

A Warner Communications Company

WARNER BOOKS EDITION

This Warner Books Edition is published by arrangement with the authors.

Cover design by Anne Twomey
Cover illustration by Donna Levinstone

Warner Books, Inc.
666 Fifth Avenue
New York, N.Y. 10103

A Warner Communications Company

Printed in the United States of America

First Warner Books Printing: August, 1990

10 9 8 7 6 5 4 3 2 1

ONE-MINUTE THOUGHTS

That Bring

WISDOM HARMONY

and

FULFILLMENT

To our relatives, friends, educators we have worked with, professional associates, students, and all others who have had a part in shaping our lives . . . and especially to our children, Steve and Julie.

— INTRODUCTION —

The material in this book has been written and developed over the past twenty-four years by our researching, reading and studying hundreds of self-help books along with listening intently to dozens of tapes.

The ''One-Minute'' thoughts compiled and presented in this book are time-tested proven ones; everyone of them has been tried and used to gain success. Many of them are easy to put into use, and in some instances practically without effort. You'll find nothing difficult in these thoughts.

They will definitely help you achieve greater degrees of success toward getting you whatever you want out of life.

The One-Minute thoughts we have set down here are not untested ideas; they are not one man's guesses and opinions; they are proven approaches to life's situations, and are universally applicable steps that work—and work like magic—some work easier than others.

Many of these priceless thoughts each represent one or two objectives of an entire book on that particular subject. As you will soon see and experience for your purpose, that depth is not necessary. Rather than reading a complete book, you will understand the main objectives from these power-packed one-minute thoughts. These thoughts for success have been reduced and condensed to the shortest amount of reading time.

There are two kinds of information: information nice to know and information necessary to know. This book only includes the necessary information on each topic.

The concept of this book can be compared to doing the math problem below:

```
   187459
 x   4165
 --------
   937295
  1124754
  187459
 749836
---------
780766735
```

You can do it the long method still used by many people today; or you can use a calculator and do it in 1/20th the time plus have less chance of a mistake. This is due to the fact that each time you multiply, add and carry over, there is a chance of making a mistake.

In a similar manner, you could read a great many books covering the traits needed to succeed, or you could read this book and have all the necessary thoughts you need to become successful or achieve greater degrees of success.

Another unique feature of this book is the fact that you do not have to make a major change in your life to begin using these thoughts to gain greater success . . . you can work into the thoughts gradually.

It is a universal fact that man is made up of what he thinks about, or what thoughts he carries with him. So it stands to reason that the more you think about something, the sooner those thoughts will stay with you. Consequently, they will become part of you.

This book has been researched and written with one purpose only . . . to make you more successful. The information presented in this book will help you more than any other book of its kind, simply because there is no one book that has all these various topics of information in it.

Richard and Janet Budzik

CONTENTS

Greater Degrees of Success

THE SINGLE MOST IMPORTANT TRAIT FOR GUARANTEED SUCCESS

There is absolutely no substitute for persistence. Consider these possibilities and their drawbacks . . .

Talent — there are many unsuccessful people with talent.

Genius — unrewarded genius is almost a proverb.

Education — The world has an abundance of educated "derelicts."

Gift of wealth (inheritance) — many have wasted it away and ended penniless.

So **PERSISTENCE** or determination is the one most powerful attribute to develop.

Golden Thread

There is a "golden thread" that runs through the life of every person of above-average accomplishment. It is the "golden thread" of Persistence.

HOW TO TRAIN YOURSELF TO BE PERSISTENT

Persistence is a state of mind which you can develop. It is based upon having some of these to an above average degree:

1. Definite purpose.
2. Definite plan.
3. Accurate knowledge.
4. Eagerness.
5. Self-reliance.
6. Will-power.
7. Cooperation, when appropriate.
8. Habit, in the right direction.

HOW TO DEVELOP YOUR WILL POWER

The most effective way to develop greater will-power is a gradual method. Too many people expect it to come to them ''overnight'' just by wishing for it or reading about it. It takes practice and concious effort. Follow these steps, with the easier ones first.

1. First, you have to recognize your problem situations--such as, sleeping later rather than taking a walk; watching TV instead of writing a letter; eating a high-calorie snack rather than a low-calorie substitute.
2. Each time you do the wrong thing, admit it and think about the improved alternatives.
3. Within a few days, start into action -- eliminate a little of the bad habit -- eat 1/2 as much of the high-calorie snack; watch TV 1/2 hr. less.
4. Every few days, increase the amount of time until you reach the desired goal.
5. Remain conscious of the bad habit until you eliminate it or have it under satisfactory control.
6. Go on to the same procedure with another bad habit.

Work at improving your will-power gradually. Don't push yourself beyond your limits of endurance -- start with a small success and grow.

THE 3-STEP FORMULA FOR SUCCESS

Nothing worthwhile has ever been achieved without constant endeavor, some pain, and constant application of the "lash of ambition" . . . usually self-imposed.

1. Use all your courage to force yourself to concentrate on the problem at hand; study it from all angles; and plan.
2. Have a high and sustained determination to achieve what you plan to accomplish, not just if circumstances be favorable to its accomplishment, but in spite of all adverse circumstances which may arise.
3. Refuse to believe that there are any circumstances sufficiently strong to defeat you in the accomplishment of your purpose.

Three Steps Needed To Master Anything

. . . Practice

. . . Practice

. . . Practice

The Power of Habit . . .

Habit is like a cable . . .

. . . you weave a strand a day until it becomes nearly unbreakable.

Good habits bring you success, and bad habits inevitably pull you down.

THE 4 ELEMENTS OF A PERSON'S "SKILL"

Your "skill" is what you get paid for whether you are a carpenter or a corporate executive, and skill is something you can develop for yourself. It is made up of these four elements:

1. Your **knowledge** is the sum of the information you have acquired.
2. Your **experience** is the testing of your knowledge by trial and practice.
3. Your **initiative** is your confidence, energy and courage in applying your knowledge and experience to new undertakings.
4. Your **ingenuity** is your ability to apply your knowledge, experience, and initiative to new undertakings.

Your **"SKILL"** is all four of these elements combined into practical methods of doing things.

12 RULES OF SUCCESS

Remember . . .
. . The value of time,
. . The success of perseverance,
. . The pleasure of working,
. . The dignity of simplicity,
. . The worth of character,
. . The power of Kindness,
. . The influence of example,
. . The obligation of duty,
. . The wisdom of economy,
. . The virtue of patience,
. . The improvement of talent,
. . The joy of originating.

- Marshall Field

6 MAJOR REASONS WHY SOME PEOPLE OUT-PERFORM OTHERS

1. *They are able to out-perform their own previous level of accomplishment.*

2. *They avoid falling into the rut of the "comfort zone" — where an employee feels "too much at home".*

3. *They do what they do for the sake of personal accomplishment, being guided by their own personal goals.*

4. *They devote their time to solving problems rather than wasting time placing blame.*

5. *They take risks after analyzing the worst consequences in advance.*

6. *They "rehearse" or think through future events and actions.*

4 STEPS TO SOLVING ANY PROBLEM:

1. What is the problem?
2. What is the cause of the problem?
3. What are all possible solutions?
4. What is the best solution?

Developing A Winning Personality

THE FUNDAMENTAL LAWS FOR DEVELOPING A WINNING PERSONALITY

You must first take the initiative in creating a friendly attitude between yourself and each person you meet. Always be a friend, and you will gain new friends. Remember these true statements and how they correlate:

1. People like to be appreciated.
2. People like to be considered important.
3. The more you like people and think them important, the more they will like and respect you.
4. The more people respect you, the more you will believe in yourself.

THE FUNDAMENTAL PRINCIPLE FOR GREAT PERSONAL LIVING

YOU are YOU. Be proud of being YOU.

Work for it and every day improve your feeling for the one person with whom you will have to live and work all the days of your life . . . YOURSELF.

Remember . . . you will never like yourself unless you know that others like you. Your self-respect must have the respect of others to support it.

5 EASY-TO-APPLY RULES TO HELP YOU GAIN THE RESPECT AND ADMIRATION OF OTHERS

These are the five easy-to-apply rules which help a person overcome resistance and gain the respect and admiration of others, through your tact and skills.

1. Be calm and pleasant.
2. Avoid arguments by using the recognized "but" method. Always agree before you disagree.
3. Treat every objection with respect no matter how trivial it may seem to you.
4. Keep your answers brief and to the point. A lengthy answer might make the objection seem more important than it is.
5. Don't repeat needlessly.

TRAITS THAT CULTIVATE A WINNING PERSONALITY

1. *Try to smile as much as possible.*
2. *Show genuine interest in other people.*
3. *Show honest and sincere appreciation.*
4. *Be a good listener. Encourage the other person to talk about himself.*
5. *Talk in terms of the other person's needs and interests.*
6. *Make the other person feel important in a sincere manner.*
7. *Arouse an eager want in the other person.*
8. *Remember that a person's name is the most pleasant sound to him or her.*
9. *Don't criticize, condemn or complain.*

ENTHUSIASM
What It Will Do For You

- Reduce or eliminate fears
- Improve your ability to easily persuade others
- Overcome any tensions
- Improve the depth of insight into any situation, job or problem
- Add a more rewarding feeling to your job and accomplishments
- Eliminate worry and fears from your mind
- Calm yourself in the fast-paced world of today
- Put new creative skills and spirit into your work
- Help others around you also have more vitality and the feeling of a winner

HOW TO GET RID OF RESENTMENT

Resentment is a type of hate and wears a person down. Try these steps to rid yourself of any current or future resentments.

1. Stop accepting the idea that you are justified in your feeling—whether true or not, it will cause you more harm.
2. Convince yourself that freedom from these thoughts is more worthwhile than the inward satisfaction of retaining them.
3. Frequently, resentments are really due to guilt for your shortcomings, or blaming others for your failures. If you are caught in this trap, admit it.
4. Prayer can help clear your mind.
5. If your resentment is centered on one person, work at changing your thoughts and feelings toward that person.
6. Look for people's good points and think only good thoughts about them.

WAYS TO HELP PEOPLE REMEMBER YOU

Emerson said: "Every man I meet is my superior in some way. In that, I learn of him."

If that was true of Emerson, it is bound to be a hundred times more true of the rest of us. We must stop thinking of our accomplishments, our wants. Try to determine the other person's good points. Always give honest, sincere appreciation. Be "hearty in your approval and lavish in your praise," and people will cling to your words, treasure them, and repeat them to themselves from time to time. They will remember you as the person who recognized them!

HOW TO AVOID GETTING ANGRY

Just saying "I won't do it again", isn't enough —

1. Keep in mind the fact that anger is an emotion, and it gets hot almost automatically. You have to work at using "coolness" to block it out — talk softer and relax your muscles.
2. Remember that an outward show of anger can make you look foolish, help lose a friend, or cause the need for a later apology—none of which are worthwhile.
3. Anger requires energy. Convince yourself to channel your anger to something more positive.
4. Tell yourself that your anger won't get you anywhere positive.
5. Use the old suggestion of counting to 10 or 100; or improve by mentally reciting an appropriate phrase, prayer or poem.
6. Usually anger is the outcome of several minor irritations with the current one being "the straw that broke the camel's back". Make a list of each irritant, and try to rid your mind of each one separately for better mind control.

HOW TO DEVELOP A MENTAL ATTITUDE THAT WILL BRING YOU PEACE AND HAPPINESS

1. Count your blessings instead of your problems.
2. Keep your mind filled with thoughts of happiness, health, hope, peace, and courage.
3. Create happiness for others.
4. Expect ingratitude in spite of helpful things you do.
5. Never try to get even with an enemy.
6. Do not imitate anyone else.
7. Try to learn and eventually profit from your losses.

P.M.A. HOW TO MAINTAIN A POSITIVE MENTAL ATTITUDE

Most people achieve close to what they expect to achieve—and most people set their expectations, or goals, much lower than they have potential to achieve. So they actually limit themselves.

The positive thinker has mental images of optimism, hope and growth through these ways:

- Maintain a spirit of enthusiasm. We have more strength and power than most of us ever realize.
- Remeber that seldom is anything you encounter really impossible. Break it down and analyze its possible solutions.
- Do not let anything ''get you down''. Overcome frustrations and irritations before they grow into big issues.
- Keep yourself feeling young in spirit with enthusiasm. Don't let yourself slip into tiredness.
- Do things for others to give yourself a good feeling through caring and goodwill.
- Have trust and belief in yourself with spiritual commitment.
- Never give up—re-evaluate your means toward your goals and maintain persistence and perserverance.
- When confronted with an upsetting situation, remind yourself of your belief in yourself to increase your courage. When grief comes, remember you or the person affected needs to be surrounded with genuine love.
- Everyone is confronted with situations that require coping—handling, confronting, and dealing with them positively.
- You have more energy and capacity for vitality in your thinking than you might realize—start using it and surprise yourself.
- A deep faith can win over all difficulties.
- Finding excitement helps keep a positive mental attitude.

A SIMPLE METHOD FOR BUILDING SELF-CONFIDENCE

The more you like other people, the more you will fulfill yourself . . .

. . . The more other people like you, the more you will have confidence in yourself.

METHODS YOU CAN USE TO OVERCOME YOUR NEGATIVE ATTITUDE

1. Practice thinking and talking only positively for hours at a time.
2. Lengthen your time of doing step 1 until you do it for an entire week.
3. Then give yourself time to think and talk ''realistically.'' It will probably be more optimistic than a week ago.
4. Practice having only good and wholesome thoughts—this will start you toward positive thinking.
5. Be with the most positive of your friends and associates.
6. Try to avoid arguments; but when unavoidable, only comment with positive and optimistic thoughts.

HOW TO LOOK UPON CRITICISM

1. Remember that unfair criticism is often a disguised compliment.

2. Analyze your own mistakes regularly and be critical of yourself.

3. Do the very best you can in spite of any criticism.

HOW TO DEVELOP SELF-CONFIDENCE WHEN SPEAKING TO A GROUP

You must first have a sincere desire to gain self-confidence. Then these ideas will help:

1. Know your subject thoroughly.
2. Have your talk, even an informal one, planned and thought out.
3. Feel and act confident.
4. If possible, begin planning a speech days in advance—this will give you more time to think about it, practice it and improve it.
5. If you think of something while relaxed before going to sleep, get up and job it down. You might otherwise forget it by morning, no matter how good the idea was.
6. Practice, not just "thinking through" what you plan to say, but actually speaking it.
7. Have more material prepared than you can use in the time required. This gives you "reserve power", that even if you forget some, you will have enough.
8. Even after experience in speaking, many people experience a slight nervousness just before beginning—but as soon as you start, it disappears.

YOUR ASSET WORKING FOR YOU 24 HOURS A DAY

You can create one asset that will keep working for you 24 hours a day among all the people who have contact with you . . .

. . . that asset is your REPUTATION.

The success of your entire life depends on the trust you gain, the assurance you create, the confidence in your judgement, and the personality which your associates can see in you. All of this makes up your REPUTATION.

HOW TO HANDLE UPSETTING SITUATIONS

1. Remain positive that a solution can be found.
2. Believe in yourself to increase your courage.
3. Remember that no situation is totally hopeless, so don't panic as it wastes time, effort and energy.
4. Your mind controls your body and soul, so keep it looking upward and outward.
5. Your mind functions better and more rationally when calm and cool — it can lead you to rational and objective solutions.
6. Practice mind control — first think of something peaceful and/or pleasant, then work into creative insights and ideas to help you out of the problem.
7. Act in an intelligent and controlled manner; overcome the impatient, desperate and panic thoughts.
8. Don't become emotional over criticism, or it can detract from using good judgment. First, analyze the specific criticism — if it is justified, improve yourself; if not, ignore it.
9. When grief comes, accept the support of those who love you.

STEPS TO FOLLOW WHEN YOU BECOME IRRITATED

- Do what you can about it, then accept it.
- Try to change or improve the other people as much as you can. Then adjust to them and accept it.
- Try to find some comfortable facets to the situation, then think about them.
- Think about the even worse possibilities, then the current situation will not seem so bad.
- Adjust yourself to take things as they come if you cannot change or avoid them.
- Have tolerance and a feeling of charity toward anyone responsible, and try to help them.
- Try to relax, think of something pleasant, to reduce the tension.
- Act outwardly as if it didn't bother you.

HOW TO BREAK A BAD HABIT

Habits are hard to break. Here's why: (1) They usually seem to fill a basic need, such as pleasure, happiness, or to releive stress; and (2) it has become so automatic it is almost involuntary or in ones subconscious. This is why many people who break one habit often find another taking its place (such as quit smoking, and start overeating).

Therefore, to break a bad habit, you must (1) analyze and take care of the need factor, and (2) plan a new positive habit to compensate for the bad habit.

All of this requires developing your will-power -- see page 5 for ''One-Minute'' suggestions. Also consider new sources of pleasure, expansion of your sources of satisfaction, re-evaluation of your goals in life, and maintaining a positive mental attitude as suggested in the ''One-Minute'' thought on page 23.

One idea in trying to eliminate a bad habit is to try the punishment-reward technique -- associate something distasteful or painful with the habit you want to break. You can do this mentally or physically. For example, every time you consider indulging in the bad habit, think about something that makes you sick to your stomach, visualize yourself grotesquely fat, or force yourself to walk or jog a mile if you do indulge.

You should soon begin experiencing the wonderful feeling of satisfaction of being in control.

Working and Getting Along With People

THE ART OF UNDERSTANDING PEOPLE

The art of understanding people can be defined as the ability to put yourself in the other person's shoes and see things as they see them. In doing this, you can anticipate the other person's desires and reactions.

This goes a long way toward your success in dealing with other people — in gaining their cooperation and making them feel good about dealing with you.

BASIC TECHNIQUES FOR GETTING ALONG WITH ANYONE

1. Never complain, criticize, or condemn.
2. Show honest and sincere appreciation.
3. Arouse in the other person an enthusiastic attitude.
4. Avoid arguments.
5. Make the person feel better about himself after he talked with you.

How To Improve Any Relationship At Any Time With Anybody . . .

Whenever you speak with anyone, always make sure they feel better about themselves, after they have spoken with you.

BASIC RULES FOR GETTING PEOPLE TO ACT FAVORABLY TOWARD YOU . . .

1. Show sincere interest in other people.
2. Smile and convey a feeling of happiness.
3. Remember that a person's name is the most pleasant sound to that person.
4. Be patient and listen. Encourage others to talk about themselves they feel good and you learn something.
5. Try to talk in terms of the other person's interests.
6. Convey to the other person a feeling of importance.
7. If at all possible, don't bring up an uncomfortable topic.

6 "QUESTIONS" THAT ARE ON THE MINDS OF MOST PEOPLE

When confronted with a new project, plan, or idea, most people have these questions on their mind:

1. How can I profit?
2. Why can I profit?
3. Where can I profit?
4. Who says I profit?
5. What can I profit?
6. When can I profit?

18 THINGS THAT EVERYONE WANTS

1. *To make MONEY.*
2. *To save TIME.*
3. *To AVOID effort.*
4. *To achieve COMFORT.*
5. *To have good HEALTH.*
6. *To be POPULAR — LIKED.*
7. *To have ENJOYMENT.*
8. *To have CLEANLINESS around you.*
9. *To receive PRAISE.*
10. *To be in style.*
11. *To gratify curiousity.*
12. *To satisfy appetite.*
13. *To have beautiful possessions.*
14. *To attract the opposite SEX.*
15. *To be an individual.*
16. *To emulate others.*
17. *To take advantage of opportunities.*
18. *To be admired.*

6 Desires That Are In Everyone's Sub-Conscious Mind

1. They want better relations with other people.

2. They want to make money and be assured of economic security.

3. They want to work less and have more chance for pleasure.

4. They want prestige, a sense of personal importance.

5. They want help.

6. They want freedom from fear and worry.

SIMPLE RULES FOR WINNING PEOPLE TO YOUR WAY OF THINKING

1. Begin each conversation in a friendly manner.
2. Be agreeable and see things as the other person does.
3. Respect the other person's opinion. Avoid saying "you are wrong."
4. When wrong, be sure to admit it immediately.
5. Be understanding of the other person's thoughts and needs.
6. Get the other person to agree enthusiastically.
7. Avoid arguments and uncomfortable topics.
8. Ignore all challenges.
9. Let the other person talk as much as he wants.
10. Let the other person feel the ideas are his (hers).
11. Appeal to each person's nobler motives.
12. Enact your ideas.

HOW TO GET ALONG WITH PEOPLE AND TO WIN THEIR COOPERATION

You can win the other person's cooperation by understanding the person you are dealing with and persuading him of the benefits he will derive from cooperating with you.

If you ask yourself the six questions listed below regarding any person you are trying to convince or persuade to your way of thinking, you will undoubtedly be successful every time.

1. *How can I profit?*
2. *Why can I profit?*
3. *Where can I profit?*
4. *Who says I profit?*
5. *What can I profit?*
6. *When can I profit?*

6 THINGS EVERYONE WANTS TO AVOID . . .

1. *To avoid criticism or being reprimanded.*
2. *To avoid the loss of possessions.*
3. *To avoid discomforts and pain.*
4. *To avoid a bad reputation.*
5. *To avoid loss of money.*
6. *To avoid difficulty.*

Studies show that people are more interested in protecting what they have rather than venturing out to something new and better.

HOW TO CHANGE PEOPLE WITHOUT GIVING OFFENSE OR AROUSING RESENTMENT . . .

1. Start by using praise and showing sincere appreciation.
2. Try to ask questions rather than giving direct orders.
3. Point out some of your own mistakes before criticizing another person.
4. Only mention other peoples' mistakes in an indirect manner.
5. Recognize every improvement, no matter how small.
6. Use as much encouragement as you can.
7. Let each fault seem small and easy to correct.
8. Help the other person feel happy about doing whatever you suggest.
9. Always let the other person save face.
10. Give the other person an excellent reputation to live up to.

TEN COMMANDMENTS OF GOOD COMMUNICATION

1. Determine the real purpose of each communication.
2. Try to clarify your ideas before communicating.
3. Consult with others in planning communications, whenever appropriate.
4. Consider any possible overtones, in addition to the basic content of your message.
5. Consider the complete conditions, including physical and human, whenever you communicate.
6. Whenever possible, convey something of help or value to the receiver.
7. Communicate in advance as much as possible.
8. Be sure your actions are consistent with your communications.
9. Follow up all communications without delay.
10. Do more than be understood, also understand — be a good listener.

THE BASIC BARRIERS TO GOOD COMMUNICATIONS

1. Lack of knowledge.
2. Fear.
3. Jealousy.
4. Prejudices.
5. Inexperience.
6. Background or culture.
7. Lack of trust or reliability.
8. Environmental distractions.
9. Ambiguous terminology.
10. Status differences.
11. I.Q. or mental ability.
12. Too much information.
13. Lack of feedback or reply.

HOW TO HAVE BETTER RELATIONSHIPS WITH FAMILY AND FRIENDS

1. Don't nag or complain—you wouldn't nag with other people, so don't with family and close friends.
2. Do not interfere with their ways of being happy—don't try to change them.
3. Don't criticize. And think twice before criticizing your children. Remember that they are not adults, do not think like adults, do not feel like adults. Talk "with" them, not "to" them.
4. Show sincere appreciation as often as possible.
5. Notice little things—they build and mean a lot to others.
6. Be polite, courteous and understanding. This goes further than money and gifts.

HOW TO ACHIEVE FRIENDSHIP AND LASTING LOVE

1. Be comfortable to avoid any strain.
2. Give the feeling that you are relaxed and do not get irritated.
3. Remember names, or people may feel that you don't really care about them.
4. Give a sincere feeling that this is where you really want most to be right now, and really want to be with this person or people.
5. Be humble, not egotistical, not a know-it-all.
6. Do not gossip, enter into questionable topics, or opinions.
7. Try to be stimulating and interesting.
8. Show understanding, sympathy, and a sincere interest in what others say.
9. At every possible opportunity, congratulate and a give a person credit for what has been done or said.
10. Help others be stronger and comfortable.

MAJOR ATTRIBUTES OF LEADERSHIP

To be a successful leader, a person must be able to get the willing cooperation of the others. These factors will undoubtedly help:

1. Self control.
2. Unfaltering courage.
3. An obvious sense of fairness and justice.
4. Clearness of plans.
5. Positiveness of one's own decisions.
6. A pleasant personality.
7. Sympathetic and understanding.
8. Doing more than is necessary or required.
9. Completeness of details.
10. Willingness to assume responsibility for one-self and others.
11. Understand and apply cooperation.

THE SECRET TO UNDERSTANDING PEOPLE'S BEHAVIOR

Indian Proverbs

"Grant that I may not criticize my neighbor until I have walked a mile in his moccasins."

"You are my friend when you walk in my moccasins."

Understanding people's behavior is an invaluable asset.

Saving Time and Being More Efficient

PRICELESS QUOTES ABOUT TIME

Time is man's most precious asset. All men neglect it; all regret the loss of it; nothing can be done without it.

- Voltaire

Those who make the worst use of their time most complain of its shortness.

- LaBruyere

He who gains time gains everything.

- Benjamin Disraeli

Time is the scarcest resource and unless it is managed nothing else can be managed.

- Peter Drucker

Kill time and you kill your career.

- B. C. Forbes

The Most Important Question
To Ask
Yourself About Your Time

What is the
best use of my
time
right
Now?

THE ART OF PERSONAL EFFICIENCY

. . It is analyzing and/or experimenting to find the best, easiest, and quickest ways of getting things done.

. . It is putting first things first; doing one thing at a time; and developing the ability to concentrate more intensely.

. . It is separating big tasks into their smaller parts; simplifying the complex; finishing big jobs one step at a time.

. . It is taking notes, and having pencil and paper do your remembering for you.

. . It is setting goals and mapping out your own program of how to reach it.

How To Keep Your Desk and Your Mind Free Of Clutter

Use these steps for each note, letter, or other correspondence you receive:

1. Look at it.
2. Think about it.
3. Make a decision.
4. Act upon it:
   — pass it on for action.
   — file it.
   — destroy it.

Don't handle it a second time unless it **really** requires further thought or consideration.

TIPS FOR GETTING THE PRIVACY YOU NEED FROM THE "SPACE" YOU DON'T HAVE

1. If your work area has a door, use it.
2. If your desk faces others, turn it around.
3. Personalize your work area with things that represent your private life. Passers-by might feel like trespassers when they see family photos.
4. These are "tell-tale" signs that you are being bothered:
   - you are coming to work early and/or staying late.
   - you find yourself going to the restroom for a moment
   - of peace.
5. If you feel obligated to be accessible to your co-workers all the time, try to make a workable change in this policy.
6. Concentrate on not looking up when others pass by.
7. If a person tries to interrupt in the middle of writing, reading, or a phone call, ignore the other person by keeping the pencil, book or telephone in hand and finish it before acknowledging the other person.

TIPS FOR GETTING THE PRIVACY YOU NEED FOR WORK AT HOME

1. Try to use a room where you can close the door.

2. Utilize any time during the day or evening when other family members are not at home or are also busy.

3. Impress upon each family member that you are only to be disturbed for explainable emergencies.

4. Make up some sensible rules for privacy, including each member of the family.

5. Don't feel guilty for wanting or needing privacy.

Explain that your need for privacy is so that you will have more and more enjoyable time with the family members . . . the quieter and less interruptions, the more efficient you will be to get your work done better and faster.

How To Double Or Triple The Work You Get Done Each Day

Each day when you start your work, first write down the 6 most important things that you must do today in order of their importance. Then do them in that sequence and make a concerted effort to block out all unnecessary disturbances or interruptions.

You will soon become amazed at how early in the day you get these things done, and will be further amazed at how many additional things you have time to do.

A FORMULA FOR DOING TWICE AS MUCH IN HALF THE TIME

THOUGHT: Think about the last emergency you encountered or the last time something had to get done in much less time than usual.

ANALYSIS: What was done differently to get the work done? Could any of those methods be incorporated into normal routine to reduce the time it normally takes to do the job? What would happen if a medical condition suddenly forced you to work only 4 hours a day instead of 8 hours?

CONCLUSION: Make a list of your most important functions; determine what you would not do, and what you could delegate. Then incorporate this into your daily work routine.

NOW you have an additional 4 hours a day for NEW and GREATER accomplishments!

5 Essential Questions To Ask Yourself Before Starting Anything . . .

1. ***Why is it necessary in the first place?***
   - *should the job be eliminated?*
   - *should it be delegated to someone else?*
2. ***Where should it be done?***
   - *could the operation be done in less time under different circumstances?*
   - *is it subject to interruption?*
3. ***When should it be done?***
   - *would some other time be better?*
   - *should it be done along with some other operation?*
4. ***How should it be done?***
   - *are obsolete equipment or slow methods being used?*
5. ***Who should be doing it?***
   - *can it be done by a less skilled person?*
   - *should it be handled by a specialist?*

Master Plan For Getting Things Done

1. Determine exactly all that has to be done.

2. Estimate the amount of time it will take to complete.

3. Set a deadline date for completion.

4. Who will be responsible for doing the work?

5. Who will be responsible for checking the work?

6. Have you picked the very best qualified person to do the job?

4-STEP FORMULA FOR TOTAL CONCENTRATION

1. Limit yourself to one piece of work, one project at a time.
2. Clear your mind of all thoughts that do not apply to this project.
3. Concentrate on positive thoughts that constructively fit into this project.
4. As your mind "warms up" to the work, you will find it calling upon new and deeper considerations and ideas.

Follow these steps regularly and gradually you will develop the habit of better concentration. This will soon result in positive plans of action for you. These plans will crystallize into positive decisions, leading you to constructive action.

TECHNIQUES FOR IMPROVING YOUR MEMORY

Most people only use approximately 10% of their memory capacity. Using the other 90% requires some conscious effort, as suggested here---

1. First, get a good impression of what you want to remember.
2. Concentrate and observe carefully, blocking unrelated thoughts from your mind.
3. Get eye impression and use as many other senses as possible.
4. Use repetition, but at convenient intervals—not all at one sitting or effort.
5. Associate it with other facts familiar to you, including people's names.
6. If you forget your next thought during a speech, repeat the last sentence or summarize the last thought while thinking of your next point.

27 WAYS TO SAVE TIME . . . . .

1. Plan the day the first thing in the morning.
2. Get up an hour earlier than normal, and go to bed early.
3. Try to do your creative and thinking items in the morning; and the things with other people in the afternoon.
4. Start with the biggest or most profitable part of each project; often the small details work themselves out.
5. Never just ''wait''; consider this an extra bonus for relaxing, thinking, planning or something special.
6. Remember that there is always enough time for the important things—if it is important, you will find time for it.
7. Set deadlines for yourself and others.
8. Don't waste other people's time.
9. Set aside specific time for ''no work'', such as weekends or evenings.
10. Review your list of current day, week, month and 5-year goals every day; determine what you should do to further any of them.
11. Carry 3 x 5 cards for jotting down notes and ideas as soon as they arise.
12. When putting something off, ask yourself ''What am I really avoiding?'' Then, evaluate the answer and try to get it done immediately.

(continued)

13. Put signs in your place of work to remind yourself of your goals.
14. Delegate as much as possible to others.
15. Consult a specialist for each special problem.
16. Learn both from successes and failures.
17. Have confidence in your own judgement of priorities, and stick to them.
18. Learn to relax and "do nothing" often.
19. Examine old habits, for improvement or for elimination.
20. Build upon successes; don't waste time regretting failures.
21. Let paper help you even when thinking.
22. Try to handle each paper only once—unless you really need to set it aside for further consideration.
23. Sometimes ask yourself, "Would anything bad happen if I didn't do this?" If the answer is "no," don't do it.
24. Regularly ask yourself, "What is the best use of my time right now?"
25. Set all "trivia" aside for one afternoon a month.
25. Always be optimistic.
27. Give yourself "time off" and special rewards when you've reached certain goals.

PLANNING YOUR DAY

The first thing each morning, make a list of all things you need to get done. Make a chart with these column headings, and duplicate or photocopy them.

THINGS TO DO TODAY

Date:

Item	Priority Sequence	Time Needed	Done

PLANNING YOUR WEEK

The first thing each Monday morning, make a list of all things you need to get done this week. Make a chart with these column headings, and duplicate or photocopy them.

THINGS TO DO THIS WEEK

Week of:

Item	Priority Sequence	Date To Do	Time Req'd.	Done

PLANNING YOUR LARGER PROJECTS

Keep this list close at hand and evaluate it daily. Make a chart with these column headings, and duplicate or photocopy them.

PROJECTS

Date:

No.	Item	Person Respon.	Date Started	Completed Date	Time Req'd.	Next Check Date

PLANNING A MEETING AGENDA

Before each meeting involving one or more other people, plan carefully. In this way, you don't waste anyone's time. List these items when planning a meeting:

1. Purpose
2. Expected outcome
3. Agenda
4. Date, time, and length.

WHAT MAKES YOU TIRED AND WHAT YOU CAN DO ABOUT IT

The brain itself is "tireless"; it can actually work as well after 8-10 hours of work as at the beginning. So, what makes us tired so we can't continue? The answer is **emotions** such as boredom, worry, resentment, a feeling of not being appreciated, hurry, anxiety, a feeling of uselessness; any of these emotions tend to create nervous tensions in the body which result in headaches, tiredness, reduced "output", and even wear down a person's resistance to colds, etc.

Mental work can also produce unnecessary tensions, primarily due to the assumption most of us have that hard work requires a feeling of effort, or it will not be done well. So we automatically use muscles to scowl, hunch up shoulders, show a tenseness.

So the answer is: Relax while doing your work! This isn't easy, but remember that both tension and relaxing are habits. Break the bad habit by forming the good.

How Long Should A Task Take?

A Task Will
Take As Long
As The Time
You Allot
For It.

Simplicity or Complexity!

You Can Make Things
As Simple
Or Complex
As You Like!

How To Motivate Yourself and Other People

TWO SELF-MOTIVATORS FOR MOST PEOPLE

1. To gain a benefit.

2. To avoid a loss.

These are the two primary reasons most people will do anything. Studies show that people are more interested in protecting what they have rather than venturing out to something new and better.

HOW TO MOTIVATE YOURSELF

A motive is an inner urge within yourself which pushes you to action (mental or physical). The most common urges include habit, mood, impulse, instinct, desire and idea. Once you realize what motivates you, work with them through a positive mental attitude. Consider these:

1. Remember that the mind can achieve whatever it can conceive and believe.
2. Things that are not probable are still possible.
3. Keep hope uppermost in your mind as the leading force in motivation.
4. You can use negative emotions (such as fear or anger) to advantage — with common sense, you can use or oppose them appropriately.
5. Be aware of the basic motives of most people -
   - love
   - sex
   - anger
   - hate
   - desire for material wealth
   - self-preservations
   - fear
   - desire for life after death
   - freedom of body and mind
   - desire for recognition
   - desire for acceptance

How To Motivate Others

You can motivate another person
to do what you want when you
give him an opportunity to
get what he wants.

HOW COMPLETE FREEDOM IS ACHIEVED

The strongest enemy you will ever face is the "enemy" within yourself. The greatest battle you will ever "fight" is the battle with yourself. The most glorious victory you will ever win is the victory over yourself. The most pleasant peace you will ever experience is inner-peace.

Epicetetus, the Greek stoic, said "The man who masters himself is free." Centuries later Shakespeare agreed when he wrote: "No man is free who is not master of himself."

To master yourself is to:

- *free yourself from procrastination, alibis, excuses, and the stronghold of negative, cynical attitudes.*
- *conquer the effects of fear.*
- *overcome perils of pessimism.*
- *transcend the ruinous roads of resentment.*

Two Reasons

Some People Make

More Money Than Others . . .

. . . Self Motivation!

. . . Stronger Material Desires!

How To Conquer Worry, Fear, Fatigue and Boredom

THE HIGH COST OF WORRY AND HOW TO ELIMINATE IT FOREVER

What is worry? It is pain suffered for something that has not happened, and probably will NEVER happen! Worry tires you by paralyzing your use of knowledge, strangling your initiative, neutralizing experiences, and stifling your ingenuity. WORRY destroys skill and creativity.

How do you avoid worry?

1. Get control over your own mind.
2. Face your problem and the very worst that can happen.
3. Analyze what you can do in a positive manner.
4. Do something about it. There is nothing like positive action to eliminate negative thoughts.

HOW TO ELIMINATE FATIGUE, WORRY AND RESENTMENT

These suggestions can help a person avoid the boredom that produces fatigue, worry, and resentment.

1. "Talk" to yourself daily to direct yourself to think of things you have to be grateful for, such as: happiness, peace of mind, security, friendships.

2. Think about becoming more interested in your job — this will take your mind off your worries, help you do your job better, and may result in a promotion and/or pay increase.

3. With these thoughts, you will be able to reduce fatigue to its minimum.

7 STEPS TO CONQUER THE WORRY HABIT BEFORE IT CONQUERS YOU!

1. Keep busy, so your mind doesn't have time to think about worrisome things.
2. Don't let small things upset you — they aren't worth it.
3. Accept the inevitable — don't try to fight or change it.
4. Consider the real importance of the thing you are about to worry about — is it really important enough for the time and effort of the worry?
5. Apply these common expressions:
   - Don't cry over spilt milk.
   - Don't saw sawdust.
   - What's done, is done.
6. Count your blessings — not your troubles.
7. Forget yourself by becoming more interested in others.

WAYS TO AVOID BOREDOM

Boredom is rare among energetic people; but when it comes, it drains you of your energy. It is frequently the result of a regular agenda that is too routine. Try these steps until you perk yourself up:

1. Alter your sequence for doing things, especially routine items.
2. Reward yourself with variety each day you complete your "to do" list.
3. Whenever possible, have others handle the details for you.
4. Be certain to accomplish a major goal each day, even if it necessitates delaying some other items.
5. Devote a half day or full day a week to catching up on the smaller items that were set aside.

5 SIMPLE WAYS TO AVOID FATIGUE AND WORRY

Applying these 5 ways to avoid fatigue and worry will help keep your energy and enthusiasm at its highest level.

1. Rest often. Rest before you get too tired.
2. Learn to relax while doing your work.
3. Apply good work habits, such as:
   - clear your desk or work area of all unnecessary papers.
   - do items in their sequence of importance.
   - when a problem arises, solve it immediately if at all possible.
   - whenever appropriate, remember to organize, deputize, and then supervise.
4. Being enthusiastic helps avoid fatigue and worry.
5. Remember, no one ever died from lack of sleep. It is the habit of worry that does the damage.

10 SIMPLE STEPS GUARANTEED TO REDUCE MOST OF YOUR WORRIES*

1. List all the facts.
2. Make up a budget that is realistic and possible.
3. Be conscious of spending more wisely.
4. Establish credit, in case the need to borrow arises.
5. Have adequate protection and/or insurance against illness (loss of income also), fire, and emergencies.
6. Don't let an increase in income cause an increase in headaches.
7. Teach your children to be careful with money; example goes a long way here!
8. Never gamble.
9. The person who does the grocery shopping and the cooking can assist greatly in being economical.
10. Don't be mad or irritated about your financial situation: think and act in a positive manner to improve it.

*Statistics show that 70% of most people's worries are financial.

HOW TO REDUCE YOUR FINANCIAL WORRIES

More worries of people are financial than all other worries combined.

Although "more money" would solve many people's immediate problem—it is not the practical or usually the possible answer. In fact, frequently an increase in income gets people into increased spending, and increased headaches. Each person or family should consider his finances as a business, and treat the topic as seriously as does a company. Nothing really new, but follow these traditional steps:

1. Write down the facts — total income, all major expenses.
2. Next, each family member must participate and list every expense for a period of 1-3 months. See how the little things add up! Doing this makes us more careful and then helps us plan ahead realistically.
3. Prepare a realistic budget.
4. Continue accurate records to show how you keep to the budget, where you went astray, and how to improve.
5. Evaluate how to get the best value for your money.
6. Don't overspend when you get an increase in income—adjust your budget and keep to it.
7. Don't use excess credit, but enough that you have a good record in the event of emergency (gives immense peace of mind). For example, use a few charge cards for convenience but pay the complete balance monthly.
8. Protect yourself and your family with appropriate insurance.
9. Have all family members participate appropriately, depending on age, to foster responsible attitudes toward money.
10. Don't gamble and expect to win.
11. Don't have resentment for what you cannot change — USE YOUR ENERGY MORE POSITIVELY.

WHAT TO DO WHEN A LOVED ONE DIES

1. Use prayer earnestly.
2. Let your feelings out — Talk, cry, be natural.
3. Think realistic thoughts — I have had my loved ones, I have precious memories, everyone has grief sometime.
4. Keep going in the same procedures, as much as possible. Do not avoid people or places as this will make it even harder later.
5. Keep busy mentally and physically, especially making other people happy.
6. Get more involved in other people's thoughts, even their sorrows.
7. Accept the conviction that the person is not lost—his existence is changed—but he is not dead. Learn to feel a sense of his or her presence in thought.

How To Relax Your Mind and Body

TECHNIQUES FOR RELAXING YOUR MIND

This generally means to reduce and eliminate your tensions, especially on busy work days—

1. Plan 1-minute quiet times throughout your day—think peaceful thoughts (a nice place to be, a family member, something of extreme interest).
2. Have at least one 15-minute quiet time each day—being free of interruptions. You may use techniques of spiritual, mental and/or physical discipline.
3. Take several deep breaths, move your arms and legs loosely to feel almost limp.
4. Clear your mind of thoughts that take energy and get you nowhere positive—including anger, dislike, jealousy, fears.
5. Visualize the most pleasant and quiet scene you know of—a place familiar to you or a picture you have seen.
6. Consider yourself as renewed mentally, physically and spiritually.

LEARN TO RELAX YOUR BODY

To relax your body, you need to also relax your mind. These suggestions work together for both mind and body.

1. Think kind thoughts, even of those who have not been kind to you.
2. Just as a person physically cleans the desk, pockets or purse, also clean your mind—of worry, annoyances, resentments, guilt, prejudices. You could visualize a vacuum cleaner pulling them out of you.
3. Think only about now—block out future plans and decisions when it is time to relax.
4. Put your mind into a tranquil mood; think of being in a peaceful picture to relax your mind and body.
5. At bedtime, do not plan tomorrow in detail, If you must, jot down some notes before retiring, then think peaceful and happy thoughts so you get the most out of your sleep.
6. If you have difficulty sleeping comfortably—put aside all problems and concerns one hour before betime. You may consider a pleasant TV show, a relaxing video movie, light conversation, careful reading, spiritual thinking or reading.
7. Think positively—I will have a relaxing dinner, a pleasant lunch, count my blessings. Relaxing the mind is the first step to relaxing the body.

MAJOR CAUSES OF FATIGUE AND HOW TO AVOID THEM

1. Avoid tiring thoughts, such as regretting failures and feeling guilty about things you didn't do.
2. Eat a light lunch so you don't get tired in the afternoon.
3. Determine the most productive hours of the day for you and do your most important work or thinking at that time (early morning for most people).
4. Set aside time for relaxing and "doing nothing" productive.
5. When unplanned "waiting time" arises, don't become aggravated; consider it a bonus for relaxing, planning or doing something special.
6. Don't delay the unpleasant tasks — get them out of the way.
7. Say "no" to non-priorities or low priorities in work and pleasure.

HOW TO RAISE YOUR ENERGY LEVEL

You have physical energy and mental energy. The mental energy is the most important consideration as it can push upward even your physical energy. The body and mind both need recharging, accomplished by rest and relaxation. Let these signs warn you:

- insulting, rude
- unfriendly
- excessively tired and sleepy
- irritable
- sarcastic
- overly nervous and excitable
- jealous, selfish
- fearful or worrying
- emotional
- frustrated
- depressed

These are outward signs of a low energy level, and can harm your health and desirable character traits. Consider these aids to improvement:

- relax, play
- rest, sleep
- vitamins, balanced diet
- read or listen to inspirational materials daily
- redirect your energy toward the most useful channels, not wasting any energy
- think energetically and show it.

When you are rested and in the best health, you are positive and have energy to direct in a positive direction.

5 BASIC RULES FOR GOOD HEALTH

Following these 5 rules can keep most people dynamically healthy.

1. Read all food labels. Chemicals in foods are not nutritious. Avoid preservatives, additives, and synthetic colors.
2. Eat fresh vegetables, fruits and whole grain products. Keep away from packaged, processed and canned foods. Vary your protein intake like lean meats, fish, beans, and low-fat products.
3. Eat more fiber foods. Vegetables like carrots, celery, broccoli, whole grain, bran products and whole fruits will give you the fiber you need.
4. Cut down on sugar, caffeine, and cigarettes.
5. Exercise daily. It keeps the blood fresh, promotes deep breathing, improves muscle tone and reduces stress.

It is impossible for most busy, modern people to adhere 100% to these ideas — but any amount is bound to help!

The Golden Rule To Good Health

Eat light and exercise regularly.

Setting and Reaching Business and Personal Goals

LOW AIM IS SINFUL . . . . .

. . . It must be borne in mind that the tragedy in life doesn't lie in not reaching your goal
. . . The tragedy lies in having no goal to reach.

. . . It isn't a calamity to die with dreams unfulfilled . . .but it is a calamity not to dream.

. . . It is not a disaster to be unable to capture your ideal . . . but it is a disaster to have no ideal to capture.

. . . It is not a disgrace not to reach the stars . . . but it is a disgrace to have no stars to reach for.

. . . Not failure . . . but low aim is sin.

Dr. Benjamin Mayes
President Emeritus
Morehouse College

The Importance of Setting Goals

Have You Set Your Goals For Today?

. . . for this week?
. . . for next month?
. . . for the year?
. . . for 5 years?

It is the person who sets for himself a definite goal and makes constant progress toward it by planning his course and sticking to it day after day without fail who eventually gets where he wants to go.

7 STEP FORMULA FOR REACHING YOUR MOST IMPORTANT GOAL

1. Decide the exact goal you want to achieve.
2. Determine a specific date by which time you intend to achieve this goal.
3. Decide exactly how you intend to accomplish this goal.
4. Make a definite and specific plan for carrying out this goal, and start on it immediately.
5. Write all this on paper.
6. Read this each morning and evening until you memorize it.
7. After committed to memory, repeat it a minimum of 6 times a day, including when you first arise in the morning and again before returning to sleep.

2 REASONS THE MAJORITY OF PEOPLE NEVER REACH THEIR FULL POTENTIAL

The majority of people stumble through life without making their dreams come true because:

1. They underestimate themselves.

2. They fear failure.

MASTER KEYS TO OVERCOME PROCRASTINATION

First, remember the 3 primary causes of procrastination: unpleasant, difficult, and indecisive things.

The easiest way to handle procrastination is not let it get started. Do these things:

1. Clarify your objectives and keep your priorities in focus; do what's important.
2. Plan early each day. Determine what you need to accomplish, how to do it, and then do it all.
3. Admit it whenever you waste time or put things off.

Procrastination can be overcome by these positive actions.

HOW TO MAKE IMPORTANT DECISIONS

What seems to be a small decision today may turn out to be a big one—looking back upon it later, it was a "turning point" in your life. Consider these ideas:

1. Go to a quiet place, sit comfortably, relax and think a few pleasant thoughts to relax your mind.
2. Convince yourself that you will make a good, or the best, decision.
3. Ask yourself what someone you admire would do in this situation.
4. Do not hurry your decision, just to get it out of the way. If you have 2 hours, or 5 days, don't rush—think about it often, think through the alternatives—each time you do this, new ideas may enter your mind and the best will gradually become predominant.
5. If still uncertain, think through the outcome of each possible decision.
6. Feel strong about your decision and act upon it with excitement. This might in some instances be equally important as the decision itself—several other alternatives might have also worked out—but how you carry it through is the real success.

Inspirational and Motivational Topics

SUCCESS

to laugh often and much
to win the respect of intelligent people
and the affection of children;

to earn the appreciation of
honest critics and endure the
betrayal of false friends;

to appreciate beauty;

to find the best in others;

to leave the world a bit better,
whether by healthy child,
a garden patch,
or a redeemed social condition;

to know even one life has breathed
easier because you lived.

This is to have succeeded.

THE MIRACLE OF FRIENDSHIP

There's a miracle called "friendship,"
That dwells within the Heart,
And you don't know how it happens
or when it gets its start . . .

But the happiness it brings you
Always gives a special lift,
and you realize that friendship
is God's most precious gift!

PRESS ON

Nothing in the world can take the place of persistence. Talent will not; nothing is more common than unsuccessful men with talent. Genius will not; unrewarded genius is almost a proverb.

Education alone will not; the world is full of educated derelicts. Persistence and determination alone are omnipotent.

Once
in a lifetime you find someone
special.
Your lives intermingle and somehow you
know this is the beginning of all
you have longed for.
A love you can build on a love that will grow.
Once
in a lifetime to those who are lucky
a miracle happens and dreams all come true.
I know it can happen —
It happened to me!
For I've found that 'once in a lifetime'
with you.

The Art Of WORK

Work brings a person to life, sets him in action. Work is a person in motion doing things. Nothing happens until a person goes to work. Work creates nearly everything in the world we live in!

The "art of work" consists of what you think about your work, how you feel about your work, and what you do about your work.

The better you think, feel and do your work, the more successful you will be.

ANYWAY

People are unreasonable, illogical and
self centered. Love them anyway.

If you do good, people will accuse you of selfish
ulterior motives. Do good anyway.

If you are successful, you win false friends
and true enemies. Succeed anyway.

The good you do today will be forgotten
tomorrow. Do good anyway.

Honesty and frankness make you vulnerable.
Be honest and frank anyway.

What you spend years building may be
destroyed overnight. Build anyway.

People really need help but may attack you
if you help them. Help people anyway.

Give the world the best you have
and you'll get kicked in the teeth.

Give the world the best you've got
ANYWAY.

STAY YOUNG

Youth is not a time of life, it is a state of mind, it is a temper of the will, a quality of the imagination, a vigor of the emotions, a predominance of courage over timidity of the appetite for adventure over love of ease. Nobody grows old by merely living a number of years. People grow old by deserting their ideals. Years wrinkle the skin, but to give up enthusiasm wrinkles the soul. Worry, doubt, self-distrust, fear and despair, these are the long, long years that bow the head, and turn the growing spirit back to dust. Whether seventy or sixteen there is in every being's heart the love of wonder, the sweet amazement at the stars, the starlight things and thoughts, the undaunted challenge of events, the child-like appetite for what next, and the joy and the game of life. You are as young as your self-confidence, as old as your doubt, as young as your faith, as old as your fear. As long as your heart receives messages of beauty, cheer, courage, grandeur, and power, from the earth, from man and from the infinite,

SO LONG YOU ARE YOUNG.

We Each Inherited Half-A-Million!

At birth, you inherited half a million hours, not dollars. You have complete control over the way you invest this time.

You wouldn't think of throwing $20 bills away. But think about the thoughtless or careless way most of us waste 25% to 50% of our time, just because we never took Time to plan how to invest enough of it!

CHILDREN LIVE WHAT THEY LEARN
Why Children Turn Out The Way They Do

When children live with criticism, they learn to condemn.
When children live with hostility, they learn to fight.
When children live with ridicule, they learn to be shy.
When children live with shame, they learn to feel guilty.
When children live with tolerance, they learn to be patient.
When children live with encouragement, they learn confidence.
When children live with security, they learn to have faith.
When children live with fairness, they learn justice.
When children live with praise, they learn to appreciate.
When children live with approval, they learn to like themselves.
When children live with acceptance and friendship,
they learn to live in the world.

Adapted

The Art Of SUCCESS

Success is discovering your best talents, skills, and abilities and applying them where they will make the most effective contribution to your fellow men and to yourself.

Longfellow once said, it is "Doing what you do well, and doing well whatever you do."

Success is mostly a mental attitude. It calls for love, excitement, optimism, confidence, humbleness, poise, faith, courage, cheerfulness, imagination, initiative, tolerance, honesty, humbleness, self control, and enthusiasm.

GIVE THE WORLD YOUR BEST . . .

If you are nice, people will say you have ulterior personal motives. BE NICE ANYWAY.

Truthfulness makes you appear vulnerable. BE TRUTHFUL ANYWAY.

If you are successful, you win untrue friends and true enemies. BE SUCCESSFUL ANYWAY.

People are unreasonable, illogical, and selfish. LIKE THEM ANYWAY.

The good you do today will soon be forgotten. DO IT ANYWAY.

People really need help but laugh at you if you help them. HELP THEM ANYWAY.

What you spend years to build up may be destroyed overnight. BUILD ANYWAY.

Give the world your best and you'll get kicked in the teeth.

GIVE THE WORLD YOUR BEST A N Y W A Y !

TAKE TIME

Take time to WORK
it is the Price of Success
Take time to THINK
it is the Source of Power
Take time to PLAY
it is the Secret of Perpetual Youth
Take time to READ
it is the Fountain of Wisdom
Take time to WORSHIP
it is the Highway to Reverence
Take time to be FRIENDLY
it is the Road to Happiness
Take time to LAUGH
it is the Music of the Soul
Take time to DREAM
it is hitching your Wagon to a Star

TAKE TIME TO LIVE

I KNEW SOMEHOW

When we sat and talked the first time,
I knew somehow that my life was changed;
your kind voice and warm touch
made me want to be closer to you.

Later, as we became closer,
I knew somehow that we would
be together for a long time;
I wanted to stop living only for myself
and begin to live for us.

As I began to live for us,
I knew somehow that the happiest
part of my life was just starting . . .
because I could be with you
and still be myself;
you loved me for being me
and I loved you for being you.

And now, I know somehow that with you
my life will always be complete,
and that I'll always
love you.

— Donna Levine

Limitations Can Be Our Best Friends . . .

The late Frank Lloyd Wright said: "The human race built most nobly when limitations were greatest; and, therefore, when most was required of imagination in order to build at all."

For example, a person plans things more economically when faced with an extreme time or money limitation.

The Art Of SELLING

"Selling" reaches beyond salesmen selling products. It is everyone "selling" or convincing others of our ideas, plans, or goals.

We "sell" successfully through a multitude of acts and attitudes. Here are some of the things that represent the "art of selling" at its best:

- *Comfort instead of coldness.*
- *Enthusiasm instead of reluctance.*
- *Facts instead of opinions.*
- *Patience instead of annoyance.*
- *Exciting ideas instead of the common place or ordinary.*
- *Remembering people instead of forgetting them.*

THE BEST OF LIFE

The best and sweetest things in life
are things you cannot buy:
The music of the birds at dawn, the
rainbow in the sky.
The dazzling magic of the stars, the
miracle of light.
The precious gifts of health and strength,
of hearing, speech and sight.
The peace of mind that crowns a busy
life of work well done.
A faith in God that deepens as you
face the setting sun.
The boon of love, the joy of friendship,
As the years go by,
You find the greatest blessings are
the things you cannot buy.

— Patience Strong

The Art Of HAPPINESS

Happiness is a state of mind.

Lincoln once said, "We are as happy as we make up our minds to be."

Happiness comes from putting our hearts and minds in our work and doing it with joy and vigor.

DON'T QUIT

When things go wrong, as they sometimes will,
When the road you're trudging seems all uphill,
When the funds are low and the debts are high,
And you want to smile, but you have to sigh,
When care is pressing you down a bit —
Rest if you must, but don't you quit.

Life is queer with its twists and turns,
As every one of us sometimes learns,
and many a person turns about
When they might have won had they stuck it out.
Don't give up though the pace seems slow —
You may succeed with another blow.

Often the struggler has given up
When he might have captured the victor's cup;
And he learned too late
when the night came down,
How close he was to the golden crown.

Success is failure turned inside out —
So stick to the fight when you're hardest hit, —
It's when things seem worst that you mustn't quit.

The Six Mistakes Of Man

1. The delusion that personal gain is made by crushing others.
2. The tendency to worry about things that cannot be changed or corrected.
3. Insisting that a thing is impossible because we cannot accomplish it.
4. Refusing to set aside trival preferences.
5. Neglecting development and refinement of the mind, and not acquiring the habit of reading and studying.
6. Attempting to compel others to believe and live as we do.

LOVE'S DEFINITION

There is nothing holier in this life
than the first consciousness of love.
Love does not consist in gazing at each other
but in looking outward together in the same direction.
To love is to stay close enough to touch
and still have enough space to grow.

Love is the willingness to see less
because it sees more.
In the one we love,
we find our second self.
Love is the beauty of the soul.
To love abundantly,
is to live abundantly,
to love forever is to live forever.
There is exquisite beauty in the heart
that cares and loves.
Love believes all things,
hopes all things,
endures all things.

AGE-OLD LAWS THAT ARE STILL TRUE TODAY . .

Government by the People . . .

.. You cannot strengthen the weak by weakening the strong.

.. You cannot help small men by tearing down big men.

.. You cannot help the poor by destroying the rich.

.. You cannot lift the wage earner by putting down the wage payer.

.. You cannot further the brotherhood of man by inciting class hatreds.

.. You cannot build character and courage by taking away a man's initiative and independence.

.. You cannot help men permanently by doing for them what they could and should do for themselves.

- Abraham Lincoln
1809 - 1865